RED FOLEY

A longtime baseball writer who worked thirty-five years for the New York *Daily News,* Red Foley presently serves as an Official Scorer in New York for both the American and National Leagues. A scorer for 22 seasons, he has worked both the All Star Game and World Series.

In addition, he conducts a Friday feature in the New York *Daily News* called "Ask Red" in which Foley answers fans' baseball questions. He is the Assistant Secretary of the Baseball Writers' Association of America, with which he has been affiliated since 1962. Foley has also contributed to several baseball books and magazines and is considered by many to be one of the most knowledgeable baseball historians in the New York area.

Red attends virtually every Yankees and Mets game played in New York.

This is Red's fourth "BEST BASEBALL BOOK".

In order to publish this book for the start of the 1990 baseball season it was necessary to prepare it during the course of the 1989 baseball season. Trades and changes in statistics and other baseball data might have occurred since completion of the manuscript, and some of this data might not be included in the book.

ALL NEW FOR 1990!

Best

RED FOLEY'S BASEBALL BOOK EVER

★ ★ ★ ★ ★ ★ ★ ★ ★ ★ ★ ★

130 PEEL-OFF STICKERS

PUZZLES ★ QUIZZES

HOW-TO'S ★ TRIVIA

AND LOTS MORE!

Little Simon
Published by Simon & Schuster, Inc., New York

Published by LITTLE SIMON A Division of Simon & Schuster, Inc. Simon & Schuster
Building Rockefeller Center, 1230 Avenue of the Americas, New York, New York 10020
LITTLE SIMON and colophon are trademarks of Simon & Schuster, Inc.
An MBKA Production
Suite 27 F, 1725 York Avenue,
New York, NY 10128
Printed & Bound in Hong Kong
1 2 3 4 5 6 7 8 9 10
ISBN 0-671-69482-0

Illustrated by Jane Lieman

To Brendan Foley

ACKNOWLEDGMENTS

Sticker and cover photos by Tom DiPace

Major League Leaders and Winners. Baseball cards courtesy of:

John V. Broggi
JKJ SPORTS COLLECTIBLES, INC.
416 Raritan Avenue
Highland Park, N.J. 08904

CONTENTS

TRIVIA QUIZ

CHICAGO
CUBS

Answers on page 94

1 If baseball had a Sophomore of the Year award, this smooth-swinging, lefthand-hitting first baseman would be a candidate for it. A .300 hitter with some home run power in his two minor league seasons, the Cubs look for the same in the bigs.

PLACE CORRECT STICKER HERE

Answer: _____

2 A longtime star with the Expos, this fine outfielder moved to Chicago in 1987 and wound up the National League's Most Valuable Player. Injuries slowed him early in 1989, but he improved in the second half and made his presence felt.

PLACE CORRECT STICKER HERE

Answer: _____

3 This lefthanded reliever, acquired from Texas for the 1989 season, gained instant fame and recognition by leading the Cubs' bullpen. A fireballer, he appeared in a rookie-record 80 games for Texas in 1986.

PLACE CORRECT STICKER HERE

Answer:_____

4 The Cubs' No. 2 draft choice in January 1986, this righthanded-hitting outfielder became an outstanding rookie with the Cubs last year. A .335 batting average for Peoria in the Midwest League in 1987 and a .331 season with Pittsfield of the Eastern League in 1988 advanced him to the majors.

PLACE CORRECT STICKER HERE

Answer:_____

Did You Know...

The Chicago Cubs, who haven't won a National League flag in 44 years, won 10 from 1906 to 1945. They haven't captured a World Series since defeating Detroit, 4-1, in 1908.

TRIVIA QUIZ

MONTREAL
EXPOS

Answers on page 94

1 A member of the National League All Star team for the fourth time in six years, this righthand-hitting infielder celebrated his promotion to the majors in 1980 by hitting a home run on his first at bat. A good gloveman, he has frequently led third basemen in putouts in a season.

PLACE CORRECT STICKER HERE

Answer: _____

2 Recognized for his glove as well as his bat, this Venezuela-born righthanded hitter has become a home run threat the past two years. He was on the National League's All Star team each of those two seasons.

ALL STAR ★

ALL STAR ★

PLACE CORRECT STICKER HERE

Answer: _____

3 The Expos' No. 1 relief pitcher, he set a National League mark for mound appearances (78) by a rookie in 1985. Two years later he was 7-0 with 18 saves, and last year he gained All Star-team recognition.

PLACE CORRECT STICKER HERE

Answer: _____

4 Acquired from Seattle in July, this lefthander fired up the Expos and their fans. A 19-game winner for the Mariners in 1987, he led American League pitchers in strike-outs three times in his five seasons with them.

PLACE CORRECT STICKER HERE

Answer: _____

Did You Know...

Bill Stoneman, now a vice president of baseball operations for the Expos, pitched a no-hitter for Montreal, April 17, 1969, against Philadelphia and another on October 2, 1972, against the Mets.

VICE PRESIDENT

TRIVIA QUIZ

NEW YORK
METS

Answers on page 94

1 The National League's home run king in 1988, this lefty-hitting longballer passed the 200 career homer plateau last year. He had over 100 RBIs in two of the past three seasons and made the All Star team for the sixth straight year in 1989.

PLACE CORRECT STICKER HERE

Answer: _____

2 The big gun out of the Mets' bullpen the last two years, this hard-throwing lefthander was credited with two of the club's three victories in the 1988 National League Championship Series. As the club's ace closer, he usually has more strikeouts than innings pitched.

PLACE CORRECT STICKER HERE

Answer: _____

3 Acquired from San Diego for the 1987 season, this righthanded-hitting outfielder has given the Mets a solid performance at the plate and in the field. While not billed as a speedster he did set a team record by stealing 21 bases without being caught in 1988.

PLACE CORRECT STICKER HERE

Answer:_____

4 A shoulder problem sidelined him in July and August, and his absence prevented this big righthander from posting his usual fancy numbers. The National League's Rookie of the Year in 1984, he was the Cy Young Award winner the following year.

PLACE CORRECT STICKER HERE

Answer:_____

Did You Know...

New York Mets' manager Davey Johnson, as a player, batted behind Hank Aaron with the Braves and followed Sadaharu Oh in Japan. He also collected the last base hit Sandy Koufax allowed in the majors.

TRIVIA QUIZ

PHILADELPHIA
PHILLIES

Answers on page 94

1 In his seventh season with the Phillies, this lefthanded hitter finally gained the National League All Star team last year. Acquired from Cleveland in a six-player swap in December 1982, he has been one of Philadelphia's steadiest producers.

PLACE CORRECT STICKER HERE

Answer: _____

2 Obtained from the Mets last June, this hustling, lefthand-hitting outfielder is expected to spark the Phillies' attack. An aggressive baserunner, his style of play can upset an opposing club.

PLACE CORRECT STICKER HERE

Answer: _____

3 A switchhitting short-stop, he has spent seven years with the Phillies, many of them contesting candidates for his spot in the lineup. Last year he showed productivity at the plate, something that was greatly appreciated by his employers.

PLACE
CORRECT
STICKER
HERE

Answer:_____

4 A longtime performer for the Cardinals, this switch-hitting second baseman was signed as a free agent by the Phillies in November 1988. He moved into their lineup and began performing at the plate and in the field as he'd done in his younger days.

PLACE
CORRECT
STICKER
HERE

Answer:_____

Did You Know...

Woodrow Wilson was the first President of the United States to attend a World Series game, doing so on October 9, 1915, when the Phillies lost, 2-1, to the Boston Red Sox in Philadelphia.

BASEBALL TERMINOLOGY

Baseball has a language of its own. How many of the terms listed below do you know? Write the answers in each box.

Answers on page 96

HOT DOG

A LAUGHER

GOOD WHEELS

PLAY BY THE BOOK

SCROOGIE

GOOD HOSE

GOPHER BALL

GRAPEFRUIT LEAGUE

CACTUS LEAGUE

CAN OF CORN

BAND BOX

DOWNTOWN

TAKE HIM DOWNTOWN

COULDN'T FIND THE HANDLE

PULLED THE STRING

TURN THE BALL OVER

A SPLITTER

WET ONE UP

A FLARE

TEXAS LEAGUER

A LEG HIT

HE ROPED ONE

HAVING A GOOD EYE

CAN YOU THINK OF ANY MORE TERMS THAT MEAN SOMETHING SPECIAL IN "BASEBALL LANGUAGE"?

LIST THEM HERE:

_____

_____

_____

_____

TRIVIA QUIZ

PITTSBURGH PIRATES

Answers on page 94

1 This former Cardinal, when healthy, is one of the top outfielders in the National League. This productive hitter, who can steal bases, led the league in three-base hits (15) in 1988.

PLACE CORRECT STICKER HERE

Answer: _____

2 A product of Arizona State University, this lefthand-hitting out-fielder, whose father was a former major league star, is capable of doing it all. He has power and speed and a fine future.

PLACE CORRECT STICKER HERE

Answer: _____

3 Originally brought to the majors by Detroit, this righthand-hitting outfielder also played for the Phillies and Mariners until being traded to Pittsburgh in August 1988. Injuries slowed him in the early going last year, but he can play the outfield and drive in big runs.

PLACE CORRECT STICKER HERE

Answer: _____

4 This righthanded pitcher was dealt from the Yankees in November 1986, and the Pirates haven't regretted the deal one bit. He won 15 games for them in 1988 and is considered one of their mound prospects for the coming seasons.

PLACE CORRECT STICKER HERE

Answer: _____

Did You Know...

The first scheduled night game in a World Series was played at Pittsburgh's Three Rivers Stadium, October 13, 1971. The Pirates defeated the Baltimore Orioles, 4-3.

TRIVIA QUIZ

ST. LOUIS
CARDINALS

Answers on page 94

1 This switchhitting outfielder has been the National League's stolen base king in each of his first five years in the majors. In 1985, his first season, he set a rookie record with 110 stolen bases and then missed the World Series because of a freak leg injury in the National League Championship series.

PLACE
CORRECT
STICKER
HERE

Answer: _____

2 Always a big strikeout pitcher, this righthander worked for the Pirates and White Sox before being dealt to the Cardinals for the 1988 season. Something of a streak pitcher, he tends to win a string of games and then has a losing pattern.

PLACE
CORRECT
STICKER
HERE

Answer: _____

3 Acquired from Los Angeles late in 1988, this Dominican-born slugger has had his career hampered by several severe injuries. Despite his many hurts, he's almost always in the Redbirds' lineup and is probably their best RBI threat.

PLACE CORRECT STICKER HERE

Answer: _____

4 Still the National League's No. 1 shortstop, this switchhitter has improved offensively the past few seasons. In addition to his Gold Glove fielding, he fits nicely into the Cardinals' offense because he can also steal bases.

PLACE CORRECT STICKER HERE

Answer: _____

Did You Know...

The lowest earned run average by a Cardinals' pitcher was the record 1.12 compiled by Hall of Famer Bob Gibson in 1968. He was 22-9 and led the National League with 268 strikeouts.

HISTORY OF THE
AMERICAN LEAGUE

The American League, like radio, television, and the airplane, is a product of the 20th century. Unlike the National League, which was formed in 1876 by a committee of owners, the American was organized and operated virtually under the rule of one man — Byron Bancroft (Ban) Johnson.

Known as the Western League, a minor affiliate in the 1890s, the eight-club circuit became the American League in 1900, and the following year declared itself a major league and challenged the older Nationals for ballplayers and fan patronage.

Johnson, a former baseball writer in Cincinnati, became president of the Western League in 1893 and later guided that group into being recognized as a partner of the National League in January 1903.

Stern, unbending, and often dictatorial in his rulings, Johnson was probably the most powerful man in baseball until the advent of Judge Kenesaw M. Landis in 1920 as the game's first commissioner. Only 37 when he began his reign as AL president, the forceful Johnson made his group successful by diligence, by eliminating rowdyism, by establishing the authority of umpires, and by the fact that he made players and managers toe the line.

Unlike early National League presidents, who served at the pleasure of the owners, Johnson virtually handpicked the men who owned and bankrolled his league. For the first two decades they worked for him, rather than the other way around.

Johnson's league was a success from the start. In 1901, with something like 60% of its players having jumped from the National, the American League had franchises in Chicago, Boston, Detroit, Philadelphia, Baltimore, Washington, Cleveland, and Milwaukee. In 1902 Milwaukee's franchise was transferred to St. Louis, and the following year Baltimore was shifted to New York where it became world famous as the Yankees.

Unlike the National, where clubs have rarely dominated for an entire decade, the American, particularly since 1921, has been frequently ruled by the Yankees, winners of a record 33 pennants since 1921. In the early going, Detroit and Philadelphia each won three flags from 1901 to 1910, and from 1911 to 1920 Boston was the ruler with four pennants. During the 1920s the Yankees won six times and added five more in the 30s. The next two decades were definitely Yankee years, as they took five flags in the 40s and eight more in the 1950s. From 1961 to 1970 the Yankees won four more, and from 1971 to 1980 added another three, a number equalled in that decade by Oakland. In the first eight years of the 1980s, eight different clubs represented the American League in the World Series.

In the early days of the century, when a million dollars was considered the ultimate in finances, Johnson shrewdly sought such millionaires as backers for his league. A key one was Charles W. Somers, a Cleveland shipping and coal magnate. Somers, virtually unremembered today, financed half the clubs in Johnson's eight-team circuit. In addition to Cleveland, Somers paid the bills for the Boston, Philadelphia, and Chicago franchises until local financing was obtained by Johnson.

Originally elected to a 10-year term as league president, Johnson was reelected for 20 years and served until ill health and a revolt by some of the newer owners forced retirement in 1927.

Johnson's later years as president saw his influence over major league baseball in decline. For a few years before the appointment of Judge Landis in 1920 as commissioner of baseball, the game was governed by a three-man committee, consisting of the two league presidents and, as chairman, Garry Herrman. Although Herrman was from a National League club, Cincinnati, he was a longtime friend and associate of Johnson. Many people thought that Johnson's influence over Herrman was responsible for giving the American League many favorable rulings from the commissioner's office. When Judge Landis became commissioner, Johnson's behind-the-scenes power weakened — a fact that hastened his retirement.

Johnson's successor as American League president in 1927 was E.S. Barnard of the Cleveland club. After his death in March 1931, the league was governed for the next 28 years by William Harridge, who'd been Johnson's secretary. Quiet and dignified, Harridge ran the American League with little fanfare but much success, and when he retired in 1959, he was succeeded by Hall of Fame shortstop and longtime Red Sox executive Joe Cronin.

When Cronin retired in 1973, Lee MacPhail, an able front-office man, was elected. He served until 1983, when Dr. Robert (Bobby) Brown, a former Yankees player and later an eminent heart specialist in Texas, took the post he holds today.

The American League, like the National, saw no franchises move until the 1950s. In 1954 the Philadelphia A's shifted to Kansas City and played there until their transfer to Oakland in 1968. A year before the American League deserted Philadelphia, the St. Louis Browns had moved into Baltimore. In 1961 the American League beat the National to expansion by going from eight to 10 clubs with admission of the Los Angeles Angels, now the California Angels, and a new club in Washington, DC, to replace the one that became the Minnesota Twins.

In 1960 Seattle and Kansas City were granted franchises, but the Seattle Pilots lasted only a year while KC is the present Royals. In 1970 the Seattle club was transferred to Milwaukee as the Brewers. The second Washington franchise moved to Texas for the 1972 season, and they currently operate as the Rangers.

The American League reached its current 14-club number in 1977, when it re-admitted Seattle and established a franchise in Toronto. Now, as the league enters its 89th year, there's little doubt how right Johnson was when, at the turn of the century, he vigorously insisted it was time for the long-established National League to have a rival, that the time was ripe for a second major league in baseball.

TRIVIA QUIZ

ATLANTA BRAVES

Answers on page 94

1 A plate slump in the first half of last season kept his bat silent, but that couldn't detract from the big numbers this veteran outfielder put up in his 14-year career. He was twice an MVP and twice led the National League in homers and RBIs.

PLACE CORRECT STICKER HERE

Answer: _____

2 Comeback Player of the Year in the National League, this veteran outfielder has played in World Series for the Phillies, Cardinals, and Royals. Atlanta signed him to a minor league contract as a free agent in 1988, and last year he contended for the National League batting title.

PLACE CORRECT STICKER HERE

Answer: _____

3 He was pinned with the National League's defeat in the 1989 All Star game, but that doesn't take anything away from this righthander's pitching ability. Acquired from Detroit's organization in August 1987, this youngster is regarded as a future pitching star.

PLACE CORRECT STICKER HERE

Answer:_____

4 This young left-hander led the National League in losses with 17 in 1988. Baseball people discount that because of the ability he displayed with the Braves last year. A Massachusetts boy, he was also drafted by the NHL Kings in 1984, but chose baseball instead.

PLACE CORRECT STICKER HERE

Answer:_____

Did You Know...

Hall of Famer Eddie Mathews was the only man to play for the Braves when they were in Boston (1952), Milwaukee (1953-1965), and Atlanta (1966-1967).

TRIVIA QUIZ

CINCINNATI
REDS

Answers on page 94

1 A workhorse out of the Reds' bullpen, this Brooklyn-born lefthander has been among the National League save leaders for the past four years. The 2.94 ERA he had in 1986 is his highest in any season to date.

PLACE CORRECT STICKER HERE

Answer: _____

2 Another of the many Los Angeles-bred schoolboy athletes to reach the majors, this righthand-hitting outfielder has been one of the Reds' top players the past four seasons. He has twice had three-homer games in his career.

PLACE CORRECT STICKER HERE

Answer: _____

26

3 He blossomed as a hitter in 1989, contending for the National League batting title. A member of the 1984 Olympic squad, he was Cincinnati's first draft choice in June 1985. This infielder made the National League's All Star team last year.

PLACE CORRECT STICKER HERE

Answer:_____

4 A lefthand-hitting outfielder with power, this youngster spent time on the disabled list in 1989. A fine outfielder, he showed an ability to produce key RBIs when needed.

PLACE CORRECT STICKER HERE

Answer:_____

Did You Know...

Cincinnati's Pete Rose holds the major league record for most years with 200 or more base hits. He did that 10 times in his 24 seasons with the Reds.

TRIVIA QUIZ

HOUSTON
ASTROS

Answers on page 94

1 He has hit more than 120 homers over the past five seasons. This righthanded-hitting slugger is recognized as the best longball threat in the Houston lineup. He was Houston's No. 1 draft pick in January 1981.

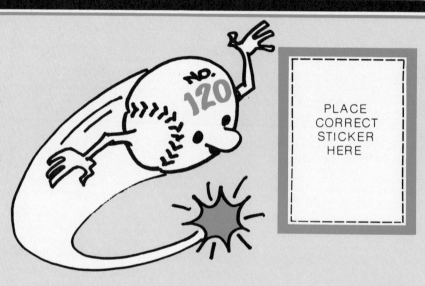

PLACE
CORRECT
STICKER
HERE

Answer: _____

2 The top lefthanded starter in the Astros' rotation, this former Yankees farmhand rebounded from shoulder surgery in 1988. In September 1986, against the Dodgers, he set a record for consecutive strikeouts (8) to start a game.

Answer: _____

3 A less-than-.500 pitcher for the Mets, this righthander went to Houston in 1983 and has flourished ever since. He added the split-finger fastball to his delivery and became the Astros' pitching ace, gaining the Cy Young Award in 1986.

PLACE CORRECT STICKER HERE

Answer:_____

4 This righthander has been the anchor of the Houston bullpen the past decade. As a result, he holds virtually all the Astros' club records for performances by a relief pitcher.

PLACE CORRECT STICKER HERE

Answer:_____

Did You Know...

Houston righthander Ken Johnson became the first pitcher to lose a nine-inning no-hitter. The Cincinnati Reds defeated the then Colt .45s, 1-0, on April 23, 1964.

TRIVIA QUIZ

LOS ANGELES
DODGERS

Answers on page 94

1

A longtime star for the Orioles, this switchhitter led the Birds in RBIs in eight of his last nine seasons in Baltimore. He was dealt to Los Angeles prior to last year. Though he got off slowly, he did show some improvement in the second half.

PLACE
CORRECT
STICKER
HERE

Answer: _____

2

The Cy Young Award winner in 1988, this veteran has been one of the game's most consistent righthanded pitchers since moving into the Dodgers' rotation in 1984. A member of the National League's All Star team the past three years, he owns the record for consecutive scoreless innings with 59.

PLACE
CORRECT
STICKER
HERE

Answer: _____

3 A former Yankees prospect, this righthander is annually among the top relievers in baseball. He starred in that role for Oakland and continued it after being dealt to Los Angeles following the 1987 season.

PLACE CORRECT STICKER HERE

Answer: _____

4 Earlier chances with the A's, Yankees, Blue Jays, Mariners, and Orioles failed to produce the desired results from this veteran righthander. His shift to the Dodgers last season resulted in a bid for league ERA honors.

PLACE CORRECT STICKER HERE

Answer: _____

Did You Know...

The Dodgers, both in Brooklyn and Los Angeles, have employed just two managers in the last 35 years. Walter Alston served from 1954 to 1976, and Tommy Lasorda has directed the club since 1977.

HISTORY OF THE
NATIONAL LEAGUE

The year was 1876 and President U.S. Grant and the rest of the nation were making plans to celebrate the 100th anniversary of the signing of the Declaration of Independence. Meanwhile a hardy group of baseball men had gathered in New York City on a blustery February day to form the National League.

Others had tried and failed to put such units together in those early days, but, as history shows, the National League, despite some handicaps and problems, succeeded.

Morgan G. Bulkeley, a prominent businessman who represented the Hartford ballclub, was elected president of the new organization, which, in addition to the Connecticut entry, included franchises in Chicago, St. Louis, Cincinnati, Louisville, Boston, Philadelphia, and New York.

Following the 1876 season, Bulkeley resigned and was replaced by William A. Hulbert, whose Chicago club had won the new league's first championship. Hulbert, one of the designers of the new league, continued to govern the National League until his death in 1882. During his term in office the league saw several franchises come and go.

Albert G. Mills, an associate of Hulbert, served as league president in 1883 and 1884, then was replaced by Nicholas Young who directed the league until 1902. During Young's final year in office, the National, at that time the game's only major league, was confronted by the birth of the American League. The two went to "war" over players, but in January 1903 they resolved their problems and have remained friendly rivals ever since.

The Nationals, a 12-club circuit in the late 1890s, dropped to an eight-team group in 1900 and remained so until the expansion of 1962. Until the Braves moved from Boston to Milwaukee in 1953, the league's cities were constant. In addition to Boston, franchises operated in New York, Brooklyn, Philadelphia, Pittsburgh, Cincinnati, Chicago, and St. Louis.

Chicago and Pittsburgh, each winning four pennants, dominated the National League from 1901 through 1910. The century's second decade saw the New York Giants win four flags; they did do it again from 1921 through 1930.

In the Depression years of the 30s, the Giants, St. Louis, and Chicago were prominent, each going to three World Series. The 1940s belonged pretty much to the Cardinals, who won four pennants, but the Brooklyn Dodgers began emerging in that decade, winning three flags.

The Dodgers, both in Brooklyn and Los Angeles, were formidable in the 1950s, winning the pennant in five of those years. In the 1960s the Dodgers and Cardinals each won three times. Los Angeles won three pennants in the 1970s too, but that decade was ruled by the Cincinnati Reds, who took the league championship during four seasons. St. Louis, with three pennants, was the biggest winner of the 1980s.

While pennants were being won and lost, the National League's business affairs were handled by a succession of men who served as its president, the latest being William D. (Bill) White, a former player for the Giants, Cardinals, and Phillies in the 1950s and 1960s.

The 1950s were a time of change for the National League. In 1958, just five years after the Braves switched to Milwaukee, the Giants moved from New York to San Francisco and the Dodgers from Brooklyn to Los Angeles. In 1962 the National League expanded from eight to 10 clubs by re-admitting New York, in the person of the Mets, and by putting a franchise in Houston.

Although they'd met much financial success in their first seasons in Milwaukee, the Braves, following a lengthy court battle, moved to Atlanta in 1966. Three years later the National League became the 12-club group it is today. It established a club in Montreal and another in San Diego and adopted divisional play, splitting the clubs into East and West units, but not on geographical lines. That's why clubs such as Atlanta and Cincinnati are in the Western, while Chicago and St. Louis are in the Eastern Division.

Further expansion has been discussed and argued but no specific time has been fixed for such a move.

Now, as the 1990 season approaches, the National League has been in operation for 114 years. As might be expected, there were good years and bad, headaches, joys, sorrows, victories, and elation for what formally became the National League of Professional Baseball Clubs that day long ago in February 1876.

TRIVIA QUIZ

SAN DIEGO
PADRES

Answers on page 94

1 A career .300 hitter who has been the National League batting titlist for three straight seasons, he has collected over 200 base hits four times. Though not a power hitter, he's a fine basestealer and owns one of the best outfield arms in the league.

PLACE
CORRECT
STICKER
HERE

Answer: _____

2 After being the National League Rookie of the Year in 1987 and hitting .300 that season, this catcher has had two sub-par seasons at the plate. Still, his great throwing arm makes him a much sought-after performer.

PLACE
CORRECT
STICKER
HERE

Answer: _____

3 Despite a power problem last year, this righthanded slugger has had big home run and RBI seasons with the Giants and Cardinals. After one season with the Yankees he was dealt to the Padres in October 1988.

PLACE CORRECT STICKER HERE

Answer:_____

4 Over the past two seasons this lefthanded bullpen product has become one of the brightest relief stars in the National League. He pitched previously for the Phillies and Giants before coming into his own with the Padres.

PLACE CORRECT STICKER HERE

Answer:_____

Did You Know...

Outfielder Nate Colbert, one of the original Padres in 1969, set a record for RBIs (13) and tied a record for home runs in a doubleheader (5), August 1, 1972, vs the Braves at Atlanta.

TRIVIA QUIZ

SAN FRANCISCO GIANTS

Answers on page 94

1 The National League's RBI leader in 1988, this former Mississippi State star first attracted attention as an Olympian in 1984. He has performed for the National League All Stars in each of the past two years.

PLACE CORRECT STICKER HERE

Answer: _____

2 His home run hitting earned him national recognition last year as the Giants became prominent in the National League West. Formerly with the Mets and Padres, this outfielder apparently found a home in San Francisco.

PLACE CORRECT STICKER HERE

Answer: _____

3 An accomplished base-stealer, this outfielder played previously for the Braves and Indians. A good leadoff batter and considered a "table setter," he signed as a free agent with the Giants prior to the 1988 season.

PLACE
CORRECT
STICKER
HERE

Answer: _____

4 The oldest pitcher to start an All Star game (1989), this veteran righthander was a big winner for the Cubs in the 1970s. Pittsburgh dealt him to San Francisco in August 1987, and the Giants have had no regrets ever since.

PLACE
CORRECT
STICKER
HERE

Answer: _____

Did You Know...

Hall of Famer Willie Mays, one of the Giants' all-time heroes, hit 30 or more home runs in seven seasons and had more than 200 RBIs in eight.

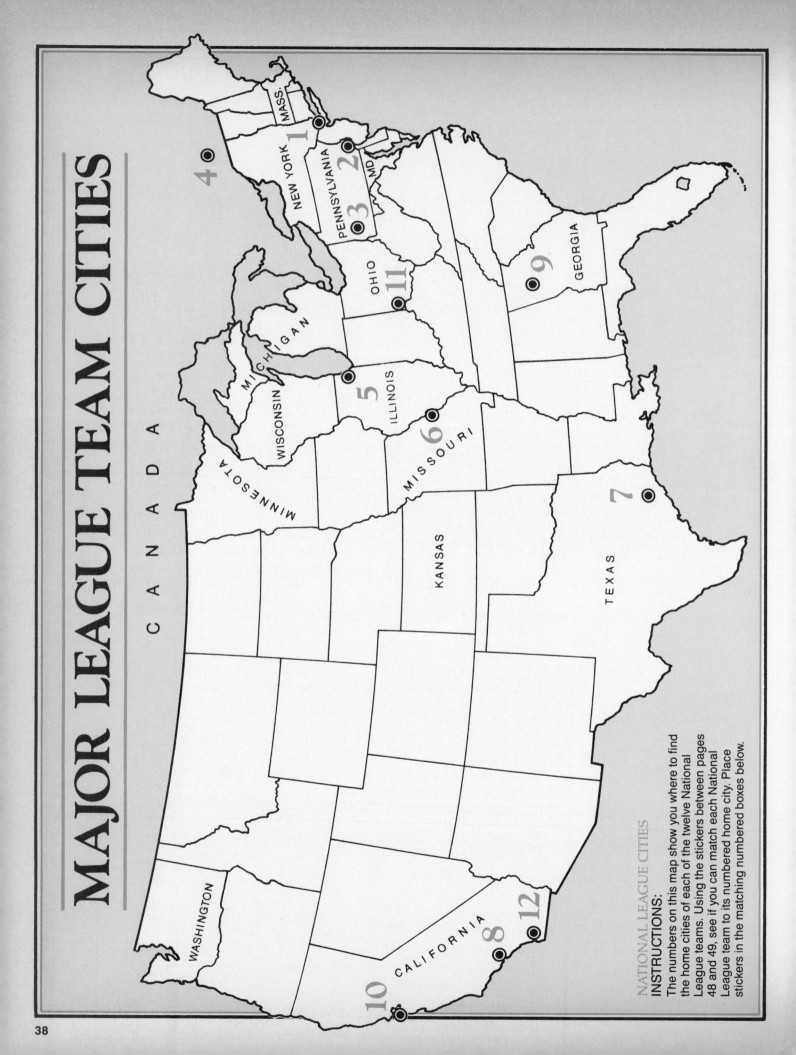

MAJOR LEAGUE TEAM CITIES

NATIONAL LEAGUE CITIES
INSTRUCTIONS:
The numbers on this map show you where to find the home cities of each of the twelve National League teams. Using the stickers between pages 48 and 49, see if you can match each National League team to its numbered home city. Place stickers in the matching numbered boxes below.

NATIONAL LEAGUE TEAMS

Answers on page 96

1

PLACE CORRECT
STICKER HERE

2

PLACE CORRECT
STICKER HERE

3

PLACE CORRECT
STICKER HERE

4

PLACE CORRECT
STICKER HERE

5

PLACE CORRECT
STICKER HERE

6

PLACE CORRECT
STICKER HERE

7

PLACE CORRECT
STICKER HERE

8

PLACE CORRECT
STICKER HERE

9

PLACE CORRECT
STICKER HERE

10

PLACE CORRECT
STICKER HERE

11

PLACE CORRECT
STICKER HERE

12

PLACE CORRECT
STICKER HERE

Now turn the page and locate the hometowns of the fourteen American League teams.

MAJOR LEAGUE TEAM CITIES

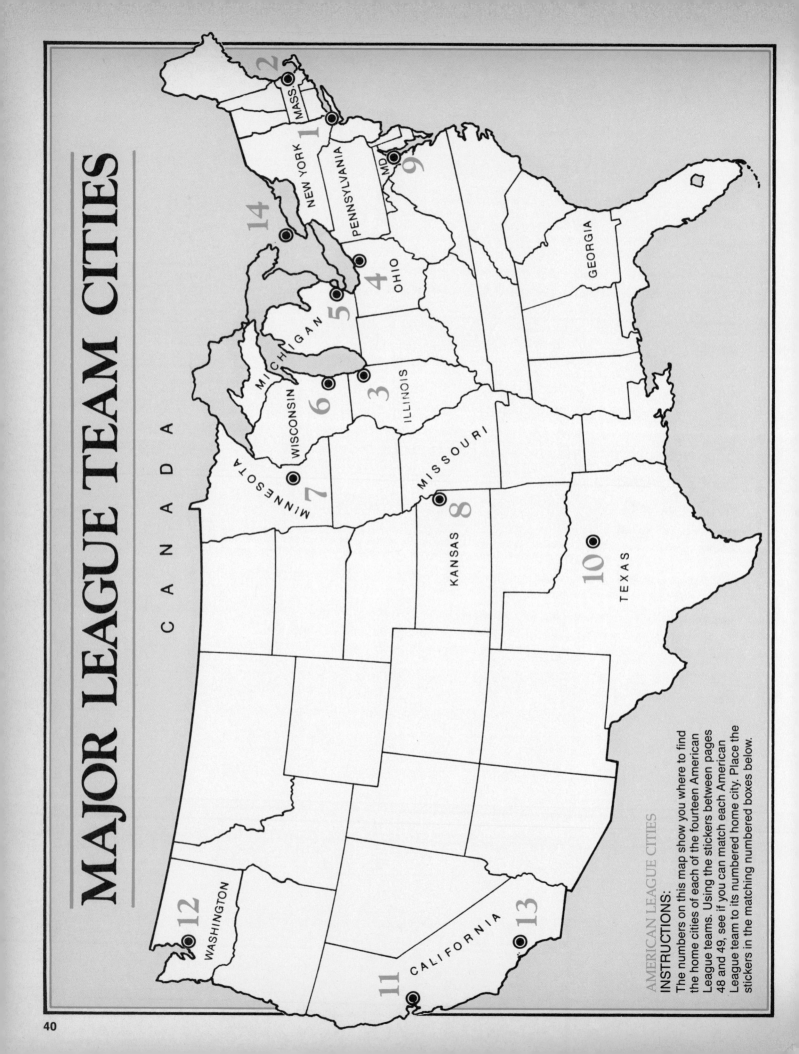

CANADA

2

MASS.

NEW YORK   1

PENNSYLVANIA   9   MD

14

OHIO   4

MICHIGAN   5

WISCONSIN   6   3   ILLINOIS

MINNESOTA   7

MISSOURI

KANSAS   8

GEORGIA

TEXAS   10

WASHINGTON   12

CALIFORNIA   13

11

AMERICAN LEAGUE CITIES
INSTRUCTIONS:
The numbers on this map show you where to find
the home cities of each of the fourteen American
League teams. Using the stickers between pages
48 and 49, see if you can match each American
League team to its numbered home city. Place the
stickers in the matching numbered boxes below.

AMERICAN LEAGUE TEAMS

Answers on page 96

1 PLACE CORRECT STICKER HERE

2 PLACE CORRECT STICKER HERE

3 PLACE CORRECT STICKER HERE

4 PLACE CORRECT STICKER HERE

5 PLACE CORRECT STICKER HERE

6 PLACE CORRECT STICKER HERE

7 PLACE CORRECT STICKER HERE

8 PLACE CORRECT STICKER HERE

9 PLACE CORRECT STICKER HERE

10 PLACE CORRECT STICKER HERE

11 PLACE CORRECT STICKER HERE

12 PLACE CORRECT STICKER HERE

13 PLACE CORRECT STICKER HERE

14 PLACE CORRECT STICKER HERE

TEAM ORIGINS

NATIONAL LEAGUE

CHICAGO CUBS

An original member of the National League in 1876, the Cubs adopted their nickname in 1907. They are the only one of the eight charter members to play continuously in the same city.

ST. LOUIS CARDINALS

Another of the National League's charter clubs, the St. Louis franchise withdrew after 1877 and didn't return to the National League until 1892. The nickname Cardinals was adopted in 1899.

SAN DIEGO PADRES

Admitted to the National League in the 1969 expansion, which brought the circuit to its dozen clubs, the Padres had long been a franchise in the Pacific Coast League. The name Padres was adopted when San Diego moved to the majors.

LOS ANGELES DODGERS

A fixture in Brooklyn and at famed Ebbets Field through the 1957 season, they became the Los Angeles Dodgers the following year. The Brooklyn club joined the National League in 1890 and became known as the Dodgers around the turn of the 20th century.

NEW YORK METS

The Mets are so named because of a contest held to pick a title for the franchise, which readmitted New York to the National League in 1962. Mets is an abbreviation of Metropolitans, a name used for a club that played in New York in the 1880s.

HOUSTON ASTROS

Houston joined the National League, along with the Mets, in 1962. Originally known as the Colt .45s, they became the Astros in 1965, when they began playing at the Astrodome, the first major league indoor facility.

PHILADELPHIA PHILLIES

Philadelphia has been a National League town since 1883, when a franchise was shifted from Worcester, Mass., to the City of Brotherly Love. The nickname Phillies is one of the oldest in baseball.

CINCINNATI REDS

The Cincinnati Red Stockings, founded in 1869, were baseball's first professional team. They joined the National League in 1876, left it after 1881, and returned to stay in 1890. The title Red Stockings was shortened to Reds for newspaper-headline purposes during the early 1900s.

MONTREAL EXPOS

When Montreal joined the National League in 1969, baseball went international. The nickname Expos was a carryover from the 1967 world's fair, Expo/67, which took place in Montreal the two previous years.

SAN FRANCISCO GIANTS

Following a 74-year run as the New York Giants, the franchise moved West for the 1958 season. The New York and San Francisco years gave the club many Hall of Fame names such as John McGraw, Christy Mathewson, Willie Mays, and Willie McCovey.

PITTSBURGH PIRATES

A member of the National League since 1887, the Pittsburgh club gained the nickname Pirates in 1891 when they were accused of "pirating" a player from another club following the breakup of the Brotherhood League in 1890.

ATLANTA BRAVES

The Braves, to coin a phrase, are a tale of three cities — Boston, Milwaukee, and now Atlanta. The Boston team joined the National League in 1876 and remained until 1953, when the club moved to Milwaukee. In 1966 the franchise shifted to Atlanta.

BALTIMORE ORIOLES

The Orioles were famous in the National League during the 1890s, and then played in the American League during 1901 and 1902. The club moved to New York in 1903, where it took a new name and eventually became the Yankees. In Baltimore a minor league team called the Orioles continued the tradition of the old club until 1954, when the St. Louis Browns franchise was moved in and admitted to the American League as the major league Orioles.

CLEVELAND INDIANS

Cleveland was admitted to the American League in 1901. The club played under nicknames such as the Blues, Bronchos, and Naps until finally emerging as the Indians in 1915. Despite rosters that contained many great players, through the years the Indians won only three pennants: 1920, 1948, 1954.

DETROIT TIGERS

An American League charter team, the Detroit Tigers own one of the game's oldest nicknames. The city had representation in the National League during the 1880s, and in 1894 joined the Western League, which in 1901 became the American League.

MILWAUKEE BREWERS

Milwaukee had an American League franchise in 1901, but it moved to St. Louis the following year. The city reentered the National League in 1953, when the Braves moved there from Boston. The Braves shifted to Atlanta in 1966, and Milwaukee was out of the majors until 1970, when the American League added the city and its Brewers to the fold as part of an expansion from 10 to 12 clubs.

BOSTON RED SOX

When the newly formed American League placed a franchise in Boston in 1901, the club, which didn't officially become known as the Red Sox until 1907, was called the Pilgrims and the Puritans. A very successful operation in the early days, the Sox won six pennants and five World Series from 1903 to 1918.

NEW YORK YANKEES

New York didn't join the American League until 1903, when the Baltimore franchise was transferred there. The team, which wasn't named the Yankees until 1913, was called the Highlanders. Baseball's most famous club won its first pennant in 1921, the year after the Yankees acquired Babe Ruth from Boston.

TORONTO BLUE JAYS

The American League expanded from 12 to 14 clubs in 1977, adding Toronto and Seattle. Named the Blue Jays through a poll, the Jays played home games at Exhibition Stadium, a refurbished football arena, until they moved into a brand new roofed stadium in June 1989.

CHICAGO WHITE SOX

The White Sox moved into Chicago as an American League charter member, the franchise being transferred in 1900 from St. Paul of the Western League. The Windy City also had the Cubs in the National League, making it the only town that has had two clubs operating every year since the turn of the century.

MINNESOTA TWINS

The Twins were new in 1961 but the franchise wasn't. They'd played in Washington, as the Senators, since 1901, before moving to the Minneapolis-St. Paul area when the American League became a 10-club organization.

KANSAS CITY ROYALS

Kansas City was represented in the American League from 1955 through 1967 by the Athletics, not the present-day Royals. The Royals joined the American League in 1969, when the league went to 12 clubs and instituted play between East and West divisions.

CALIFORNIA ANGELS

Originally named the Los Angeles Angels when they came into the American League as an expansion club in 1961, the team moved downstate to their own ballpark in Anaheim in 1965 and became the California Angels.

OAKLAND ATHLETICS

Originally the Philadelphia A's from 1901 through 1954, the franchise was moved to Kansas City. Then in 1968 the team moved further West to Oakland, where it has been operating ever since.

SEATTLE MARINERS

When the American League became a 14-club organization in 1977, Seattle was one of the new members. Known as the Mariners from the outset, the Seattle team began play in a domed stadium, the first such ballpark in the American League.

TEXAS RANGERS

The Rangers came into being in 1972, when the club was moved from Washington, DC, where since 1961 it had been known as the Senators. The Washington Senators were themselves replacements for a team that had moved to Minnesota in 1961 to become the Twins.

TRIVIA QUIZ

BALTIMORE ORIOLES

Answers on page 94

1 The American League's All Star shortstop the past seven years, this righthand-hitting star blends power with timely hitting. Rookie of the Year in 1982, he was the league's MVP the following season and is making a bid to challenge the mark for playing consecutive games.

PLACE CORRECT STICKER HERE

Answer: _____

2 This switchhitting catcher had several unsuccessful trials with Oakland before being signed by the Orioles as a free agent in April 1988. The Birds used him in 86 games that season. Last year he hit the longball and led the club in home runs.

PLACE CORRECT STICKER HERE

Answer: _____

3 The Orioles surprised a lot of clubs in 1989, and this southpaw was one of the chief reasons why. Signed out of Stanford University in 1985, he had two losing seasons in 1987 and 1988 before putting it together last year.

PLACE CORRECT STICKER HERE

Answer:_____

4 Baltimore's first-round draft pick in June 1988, this former Auburn University righthander pitched a mere 24.1 minor league innings before being advanced to the parent club. Last year he was placed in the bullpen and wound up leading the Birds' staff in saves.

PLACE CORRECT STICKER HERE

Answer:_____

Did You Know...

Future Hall of Fame righthander Jim Palmer was a 20-game winner for the Baltimore Orioles in eight of nine seasons from 1970 to 1978.

STICKER NUMBERS

On the next pages are the stickers for the answers to the Trivia Quizzes. This list shows the sticker numbers and each player's name.

1.	Allan Anderson	27.	Doug Drabek
2.	Scott Bailes	28.	Lenny Dykstra
3.	Jeff Ballard	29.	Dennis Eckersley
4.	Jesse Barfield	30.	Steve Farr
5.	Bert Blyleven	31.	Tony Fernandez
6.	Wade Boggs	32.	Carlton Fisk
7.	Barry Bonds	33.	John Franco
8.	Chris Bosio	34.	Julio Franco
9.	George Brett	35.	Andres Galarraga
10.	Tim Burke	36.	Tom Glavine
11.	Ellis Burks	37.	Dwight Gooden
12.	Brett Butler	38.	Mark Grace
13.	Ivan Calderon	39.	Mike Greenwell
14.	Jose Canseco	40.	Ken Griffey, Jr.
15.	Joe Carter	41.	Kelly Gruber
16.	Jack Clark	42.	Pedro Guerrero
17.	Will Clark	43.	Tony Gwynn
18.	Roger Clemens	44.	Bryan Harvey
19.	Vince Coleman	45.	Von Hayes
20.	Eric Davis	46.	Willie Hernandez
21.	Glenn Davis	47.	Tommy Herr
22.	Mark Davis	48.	Orel Hershiser
23.	Andre Dawson	49.	Jay Howell
24.	Rob Deer	50.	Kent Hrbek
25.	Jose DeLeon	51.	Bo Jackson
26.	Jim Deshaies	52.	Steve Jeltz

53.	Jimmy Key	79.	Dave Righetti
54.	Ron Kittle	80.	Jeff Russell
55.	Mark Langston	81.	Nolan Ryan
56.	Carney Lansford	82.	Benito Santiago
57.	Barry Larkin	83.	Steve Sax
58.	Jeffrey Leonard	84.	Mike Schooler
59.	Don Mattingly	85.	Mike Scott
60.	Fred McGriff	86.	Kevin Seitzer
61.	Mark McGwire	87.	Dave Smith
62.	Kevin McReynolds	88.	Lonnie Smith
63.	Randy Myers	89.	Ozzie Smith
64.	Kevin Mitchell	90.	John Smoltz
65.	Paul Molitor	91.	Cory Snyder
66.	Mike Morgan	92.	Daryl Strawberry
67.	Dale Murphy	93.	Greg Swindell
68.	Eddie Murray	94.	Mickey Tettleton
69.	Matt Nokes	95.	Bobby Thigpen
70.	Greg Olson	96.	Alan Trammell
71.	Paul O'Neill	97.	Dave Valle
72.	Rafael Palmeiro	98.	Andy Van Slyke
73.	Lance Parrish	99.	Tim Wallach
74.	Dan Plesac	100.	Jerome Walton
75.	Kirby Puckett	101.	Lou Whitaker
76.	Jeff Reardon	102.	Devon White
77.	Rick Reuschel	103.	Mitch Williams
78.	Cal Ripken	104.	Glenn Wilson

TRIVIA QUIZ

BOSTON
RED SOX

Answers on page 94

1 Despite failing to win his fifth consecutive batting title, this infielder did exceed .300 for the eighth straight year in 1989. Not advertised as a slugger or longball producer, he hit a homer in the 1989 All Star game.

PLACE CORRECT STICKER HERE

Answer: _____

2 One of baseball's best young hitters for average, this lefty-swinging outfielder has both long-ball and RBI abilities. In 1988, his second full season, he led the league with a record 23 game-winning RBIs.

PLACE CORRECT STICKER HERE

Answer: _____

3 Boston's first-round draft choice in January 1983, this outfielder is highly desired by rival teams and often mentioned in trade talks. A multi-threat performer with fine offensive and defensive abilities, he is also a good basestealer.

PLACE CORRECT STICKER HERE

Answer: _____

4 The American League's Cy Young Award winner in 1986 and 1987, this righthander led the league in strikeouts with 291 in 1988. In 1986, his first 20-victory season, he set a major league record with 20 strikeouts against the Mariners, April 29, at Boston.

PLACE CORRECT STICKER HERE

Answer: _____

Did You Know...

Babe Ruth (1916-1917), Lefty Grove (1935), and Mel Parnell (1949, 1953) are the only southpaws to enjoy 20-victory seasons pitching for the Boston Red Sox.

Starting Lineup of the
1989 ALL STAR TEAM

NATIONAL LEAGUE

Will Clark, Giants 1b

Ryne Sandberg, Cubs 2b

Howard Johnson, Mets 3b

Ozzie Smith, Cardinals . . . . ss

Kevin Mitchell, Giants . . . . lf

Eric Davis, Reds . . . . cf

Tony Gwynn, Padres . . . . rf

Rick Reuschel, Giants . . . . p

Benito Santiago, Padres c

Pedro Guerrero, Cardinals . . . . dh

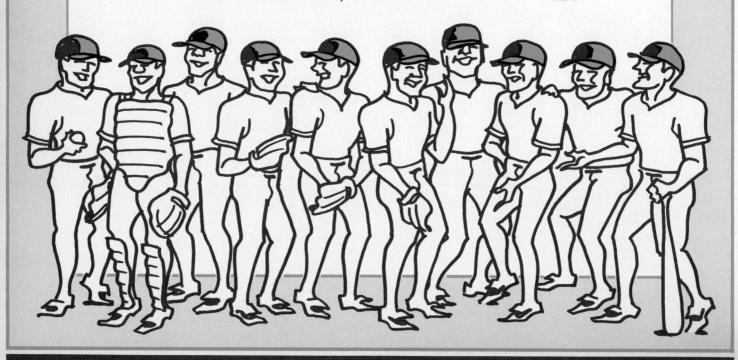

AMERICAN LEAGUE

Mark McGwire, A's 1b

Julio Franco, Rangers 2b

Wade Boggs, Red Sox 3b

Cal Ripken, Jr., Orioles . . . . ss

Bo Jackson, Royals . . . . lf

Kirby Puckett, Twins . . . . cf

Ruben Sierra, Rangers . . . . rf

Dave Stewart, A's . . . . p

Terry Steinback, A's c

Harold Baines, White Sox . . . . dh

TRIVIA QUIZ

CLEVELAND
INDIANS

Answers on page 94

1 Dealt to Cleveland by the Cubs in June 1984, this righthand-hitting outfielder has been one of the Tribe's best. He led the American League in RBIs with 121 in 1986, and last year tied a major league record for home runs in two consecutive games.

PLACE CORRECT STICKER HERE

Answer: _____

2 A former Olympian, this righthand-hitting outfielder was the Indians' No. 1 draft pick in June 1984. A home run producer, he also owns what many baseball people regard as the best throwing arm in the American League.

PLACE CORRECT STICKER HERE

Answer: _____

3 Drafted No. 1 by the Indians in June 1986, this Texas University lefthander pitched only 18 minor league innings before being brought to Cleveland. A .500 pitcher in 1986 and 1987, he won 18 the next year and continued to display talent last season.

Answer: _____

4 This young lefthander, acquired from the Pittsburgh organization in 1985, has shown flashes of mound brilliance. However, like so many southpaws, it's going to take him a little more time to develop fully.

Answer: _____

Did You Know...

The Cleveland Indians have retired only three uniform numbers — Bob Feller (19), Lou Boudreau (5), and Earl Averill (3).

TRIVIA QUIZ

DETROIT
TIGERS

Answers on page 94

1 This classy infielder was the American League's Rookie of the Year in 1978. He has been one of the Tigers' best ever since. Though never considered a longball threat, this lefty swinger had a career high in homers last year.

PLACE CORRECT STICKER HERE

Answer:_____

2 This veteran southpaw reliever rebounded nicely after having what was considered sub-par seasons in 1987 and 1988. His memorable year was 1984, when the Tigers won it all and he took both the Cy Young and MVP prizes.

PLACE CORRECT STICKER HERE

Answer:_____

3 Injuries restricted this lefthand-hitting catcher's activity in the first half of last season. As a result his numbers weren't that noticeable. In 1987, his first full year, he hit 32 homers while serving as the backup catcher.

PLACE CORRECT STICKER HERE

Answer: _____

4 A star shortstop for more than a decade, this righthand-hitting infielder has batted over .300 five times and has been named to the American League All Star team on five occasions. Injuries slowed him down in 1989.

PLACE CORRECT STICKER HERE

Answer: _____

Did You Know...

Detroit manager Sparky Anderson is the only skipper to win World Series championships in each league. He did it with Cincinnati (1975 and 1976) and with the Tigers in 1984.

TRIVIA QUIZ

MILWAUKEE
BREWERS

Answers on page 94

1 One of the keys in the Brewers' offense the past dozen seasons, this infielder and sometime designated hitter set a World Series record by collecting five hits in a Series game in 1982.

PLACE CORRECT STICKER HERE

Answer: _____

2 Despite a high number of strikeouts, this outfielder has been one of Milwaukee's top home run producers, with many of his shots being termed "tape-measure" drives. He was acquired from the Giants in December 1985.

PLACE CORRECT STICKER HERE

Answer: _____

3 He is one of the American League's top relief pitchers. This fireballing southpaw, a member of the American League's All Star team last year, has been the Brewers' most consistent fireman since reaching the majors in 1986.

PLACE
CORRECT
STICKER
HERE

Answer:_____

4 Employed both as a starter and reliever in 1988, this righthander became a part of Milwaukee's mound rotation last year. He displayed his ability to produce both strike-outs and victories.

PLACE
CORRECT
STICKER
HERE

Answer:_____

Did You Know...

Righthanded reliever Rollie Fingers (1981) and shortstop Robin Yount (1982) are the only Milwaukee Brewers to win the Most Valuable Player award.

TRIVIA QUIZ

NEW YORK YANKEES

Answers on page 94

1 A perennial member of the American League's All Star squad, this lefthanded first baseman is annually one of the game's top performers at the plate and in the field. A career .300 hitter, he won the AL batting title in 1984.

PLACE CORRECT STICKER HERE

Answer: _____

2 A longtime star with the Dodgers, this infielder signed with the Yankees as a free agent last year. It was one of the club's best moves because he proved to be adequate not only at the plate but in the field.

PLACE CORRECT STICKER HERE

Answer: _____

3 A no-hit pitcher in 1983, this lefthander shifted to the bullpen the following year, and his production ever since has made the move a good one. He was the American League's Rookie of the Year in 1981.

PLACE CORRECT STICKER HERE

Answer: _____

4 Acquired from Toronto last May, this righthanded-hitting outfielder has what many consider the best throwing arm in the American League. In addition he is a longball hitter and in 1986 had a career high 40 homers.

PLACE CORRECT STICKER HERE

Answer: _____

Did You Know...

The Yankees have won the most pennants (33) and World Series (22), but they played 18 years in New York before winning their first flag (1921) and 20 years before winning their first Series (1923).

Most Valuable Player

NATIONAL LEAGUE

1980
Mike Schmidt
Philadelphia

1981
Mike Schmidt
Philadelphia

1982
Dale Murphy
Atlanta

1983
Dale Murphy
Atlanta

1984
Ryne Sandberg
Chicago

1985
Willie McGee
St. Louis

1986
Mike Schmidt
Philadelphia

1987
Andre Dawson
Chicago

1988
Kirk Gibson
Los Angeles

1989 Winner _____
(fill in name)

AMERICAN LEAGUE

1980
George Brett
Kansas City

1981
Rollie Fingers
Milwaukee

1982
Robin Yount
Milwaukee

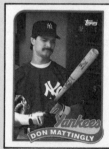

1983
Cal Ripken, Jr.
Baltimore

1984
Willie Hernandez
Detroit

1985
Don Mattingly
New York

1986
Roger Clemens
Boston

1987
George Bell
Toronto

1988
Jose Canseco
Oakland

1989 Winner _____
(fill in name)

The players shown below have been awarded top honors in the decade of the 80's. Fill in the champions for 1989.

Rookie of the Year Award
(Baseball Writer's Association of America)

| NATIONAL LEAGUE | | | AMERICAN LEAGUE | | |

NATIONAL LEAGUE | ## AMERICAN LEAGUE

| 1980 | 1981 | 1982 | 1980 | 1981 | 1982 |
| Steve Howe
Los Angeles | Fernando Valenzuela
Los Angeles | Steve Sax
Los Angeles | Joe Charboneau
Cleveland | Dave Righetti
New York | Cal Ripken, Jr.
Baltimore |

| 1983 | 1984 | 1985 | 1983 | 1984 | 1985 |
| Darryl Strawberry
New York | Dwight Gooden
New York | Vince Coleman
St. Louis | Ron Kittle
Chicago | Alvin Davis
Seattle | Ozzie Guillen
Chicago |

| 1986 | 1987 | 1988 | 1986 | 1987 | 1988 |
| Todd Worrell
St. Louis | Benito Santiago
San Diego | Chris Sabo
Cincinnati | Jose Canseco
Oakland | Mark McGwire
Oakland | Walt Weiss
Oakland |

1989 Winner _____

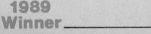

(fill in name)

1989 Winner _____

(fill in name)

Cy Young Award

NATIONAL LEAGUE

1980
Steve Carlton
Philadelphia

1981
Fernando Valenzuela
Los Angeles

1982
Steve Carlton
Philadelphia

1983
John Denny
Philadelphia

1984
Rick Sutcliffe
Chicago

1985
Dwight Gooden
New York

1986
Mike Scott
Houston

1987
Steve Bedrosian
Philadelphia

1988
Orel Hershiser
Los Angeles

1989 Winner _____
(fill in name)

AMERICAN LEAGUE

1980
Steve Stone
Baltimore

1981
Rollie Fingers
Milwaukee

1982
Pete Vuckovich
Milwaukee

1983
LaMarr Hoyt
Chicago

1984
Willie Hernandez
Detroit

1985
Bret Saberhagen
Kansas City

1986
Roger Clemens
Boston

1987
Roger Clemens
Boston

1988
Frank Viola
Minnesota

1989 Winner _____
(fill in name)

Batting Champions

NATIONAL LEAGUE

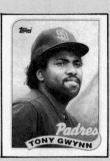

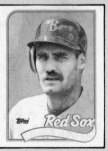
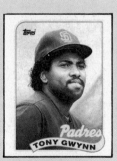
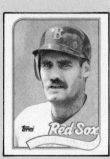

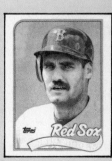
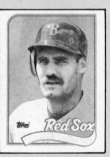

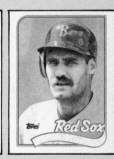

1980
Bill Buckner
Chicago .324

1981
Bill Madlock
Pittsburgh .341

1982
Al Oliver
Montreal .331

1983
Bill Madlock
Pittsburgh .323

1984
Tony Gwynn
San Diego .351

1985
Willie McGee
St. Louis .353

1986
Tim Raines
Montreal .334

1987
Tony Gwynn
San Diego .370

1988
Tony Gwynn
San Diego .313

1989 Champion _____

(fill in name)

AMERICAN LEAGUE

1980
George Brett
Kansas City .390

1981
Carney Lansford
Boston .336

1982
Willie Wilson
Kansas City .332

1983
Wade Boggs
Boston .361

1984
Don Mattingly
New York .343

1985
Wade Boggs
Boston .368

1986
Wade Boggs
Boston .357

1987
Wade Boggs
Boston .363

1988
Wade Boggs
Boston .366

1989 Champion _____

(fill in name)

Major League
Home Run Champions

NATIONAL LEAGUE

1980
Mike Schmidt
Philadelphia, 48

1981
Mike Schmidt
Philadelphia, 31

1982
Dave Kingman
New York, 37

1983
Mike Schmidt
Philadelphia, 40

1984
Dale Murphy
Atlanta, 36

1984
Mike Schmidt
Philadelphia, 36

1985
Dale Murphy
Atlanta, 37

1986
Mike Schmidt
Philadelphia, 37

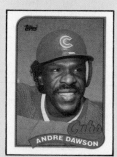

1987
Andre Dawson
Chicago, 49

1988
Darryl Strawberry
New York, 39

1989 Champion _____

(fill in name)

AMERICAN LEAGUE

1980
Reggie Jackson
New York, 41

1980
Ben Ogilvie
Milwaukee, 41

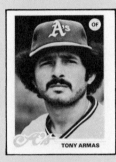

1981
Tony Armas
Oakland, 22

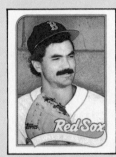

1981
Dwight Evans
Boston, 22

1981
Bobby Grich
California, 22

1981
Eddie Murray
Baltimore, 22

1982
Reggie Jackson
California, 39

1982
Gorman Thomas
Milwaukee, 39

1983
Jim Rice
Boston, 39

1984
Tony Armas
Boston, 43

1985
Darrell Evans
Detroit, 40

1986
Jesse Barfield
Toronto, 40

1987
Mark McGwire
Oakland, 49

1988
Jose Canseco
Oakland, 42

1989 Champion _____

(fill in name)

TRIVIA QUIZ

TORONTO BLUE JAYS

Answers on page 94

1 One of the American League's better lefthanders, this former Clemson University performer won 17 games for Toronto in 1987. The following year, after arm surgery, he won a dozen games despite only 21 mound appearances.

PLACE CORRECT STICKER HERE

Answer: _____

2 He has been something of a jack-of-all-trades infielder and outfielder since coming to the Blue Jays in 1984. This righthanded batter's performance was finally recognized when he was added to the American League's All Star team last year.

PLACE CORRECT STICKER HERE

Answer: _____

3 He is probably the most acrobatic shortstop in the American League. This switchhitting Dominican, whom Toronto first signed at age 17, has made the All Star team in three of the past four years.

PLACE CORRECT STICKER HERE

Answer: _____

4 This lefty-hitting longballer is the Blue Jays' No. 1 home run threat. Toronto acquired him in a 1982 trade with the Yankees. He proved his versatility by leading American League first basemen in fielding percentage in 1988.

PLACE CORRECT STICKER HERE

Answer: _____

Did You Know...

Catcher Ernie Whitt was selected from Boston in the November 1976 expansion draft as one of 30 players chosen by the new Toronto team. He is the only one of those players to perform for the Blue Jays in each of their 13 seasons (1977-1989) in the American League.

TRIVIA QUIZ

CALIFORNIA ANGELS

Answers on page 94

1 Named the All Star catcher no fewer than seven times since 1980, this former Tigers star played two years with the Phillies before being dealt to the Angels in October 1988.

PLACE CORRECT STICKER HERE

Answer: _____

2 He became one of the American League's top relief artists in only his second full season with the Angels. This righthanded strikeout specialist has more Ks than innings pitched the past two years.

PLACE CORRECT STICKER HERE

Answer: _____

3 This switchhitting Jamaica-born outfielder has shown great basestealing and longball-hitting ability since becoming a regular in the California outfield in 1987.

PLACE CORRECT STICKER HERE

Answer:_____

4 A 20-season veteran of both leagues, this righthander is No. 2 in lifetime strikeouts among active pitchers. The many years he has worked have sharpened his great curveball.

PLACE CORRECT STICKER HERE

Answer:_____

Did You Know...

Alex Johnson, who edged Boston's Carl Yastrzemski .3289 to .3286 in 1970, is the only California Angels player to win an American League batting title.

TRIVIA QUIZ

WHITE SOX

CHICAGO
WHITE SOX

Answers on page 94

1 This veteran catcher collected his 2,000th career base hit last July. Despite being sidelined by injuries the past season, he has put up what many consider Hall of Fame numbers in his 20 years in the American League.

PLACE CORRECT STICKER HERE

Answer: _____

2 Serious back surgery hampered him in 1989, but Sox fans are confident that this sometime outfielder, mostly designated hitter, will regain the longball form that has made him a Chicago favorite.

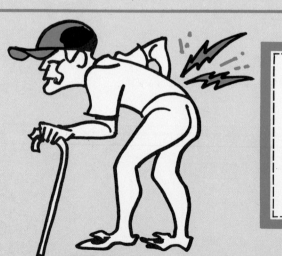

PLACE CORRECT STICKER HERE

Answer: _____

3 Acquired from Seattle in July 1986, this outfielder has hit 10 or more home runs in each of the past three seasons for the White Sox.

PLACE CORRECT STICKER HERE

Answer:_____

4 The No. 1 man out of the White Sox bullpen for the past three years, this hard-throwing righthander set a club mark with 34 saves in 1988. He should establish several mound marks in the future.

BULLPEN

PLACE CORRECT STICKER HERE

Answer:_____

Did You Know...

Comiskey Park, which has housed White Sox teams since July 1, 1910, is the oldest ballpark in the major leagues.

BIRTH CERTIFICATE
COMISKY PARK 1910

TRIVIA QUIZ

KANSAS CITY
ROYALS

Answers on page 94

1 A veteran of 10 All Star games, this career .300 hitter has won two American League batting titles. One was with a .390 average, the highest compiled in the majors in the decade of the 1980s.

PLACE CORRECT STICKER HERE

Answer: _____

2 This infielder is the first Royals' rookie to collect 200 hits in a season — 207 in 1987. His abilities at the plate and with the glove enabled Kaycee to shift longtime third baseman George Brett to first base.

PLACE CORRECT STICKER HERE

Answer: _____

3 His feats as a longball-hitting outfielder really blossomed in 1989. His All Star game homer added to the athletic laurels he has been earning as both a baseball and pro football player.

PLACE CORRECT STICKER HERE

Answer: _____

4 Kansas City's top relief pitcher in each of the past two seasons, this right-handed strikeout artist was the property of Cleveland and Pittsburgh before signing with the Royals as a free agent in 1985.

PLACE CORRECT STICKER HERE

Answer: _____

Did You Know...

George Brett's league-leading .390 batting average for the Kansas City Royals in 1980 was the highest average a major leaguer has compiled since Boston's Ted Williams hit .406 in 1941.

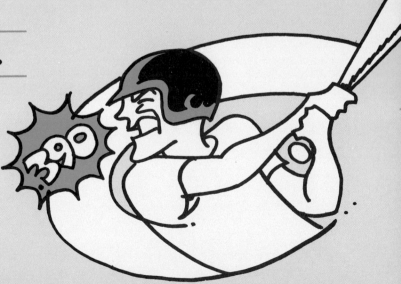

COLLECTING BASEBALL CARDS

Here is a list of popular and valuable baseball cards from the early 1900s to today. The name of the card company and the year the card was issued appear beneath the player's picture. Values are for cards in mint condition. How many of these players do you know?

JOE JACKSON
1909 American Caramel
Listed at $750.

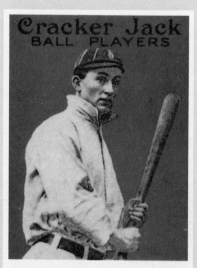

TY COBB
1914 Cracker Jack
Listed at $2,500.

HONUS WAGNER
1909 T206
Listed at $90,000.

BABE RUTH
1933 Goudy
Listed at $2,400

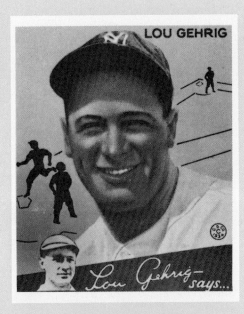

LOU GEHRIG
1934 Goudy
Listed at $1,750.

CARL HUBBELL
1934 Goudy
Listed at $175.

WILLIE MAYS
1953 Topps
Listed at $1,400.

STAN MUSIAL
1955 Rawlings
Listed at $150.

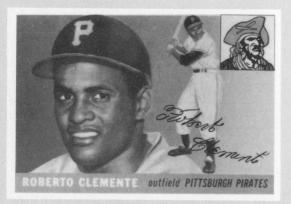

ROBERTO CLEMENTE
1955 Topps
Listed at $750.

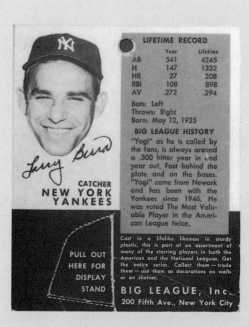

YOGI BERRA
1955 Big League
Listed at $125.

DODGER SLUGGERS
1957 Topps
Listed at $150.

YANKEE POWER HITTERS
1957 Topps
Listed at $250.

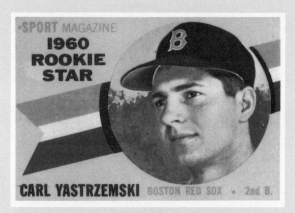

CARL YASTRZEMSKI
1960 Topps
Listed at $250.

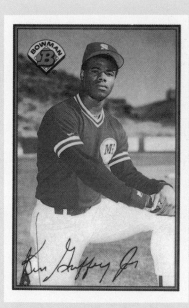

KEN GRIFFEY, JR.
1989 Bowman
Listed at $5 (hottest card today).

TED WILLIAMS
1939 Gum Inc.
Listed at $1,000.

JOE DIMAGGIO
1941 Gum Inc.
Listed at $1,350.

SATCHEL PAIGE
1949 Leaf
Listed at $1,650.

BOB FELLER
1949 Leaf
Listed at $1,000.

JACKIE ROBINSON
1950 Bowman
Listed at $450.

MICKEY MANTLE
1951 Bowman
Listed at $5,500.

ROBIN ROBERTS
1951 Topps "Current All Star"
Listed at $9,000.

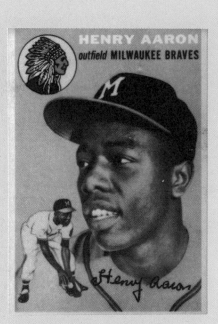

HANK AARON
1954 Topps
Listed at $800.

TRIVIA QUIZ

MINNESOTA
TWINS

Answers on page 94

1 His 2.45 ERA in 1988 made him the American League leader in earned run average, the first time a Twins pitcher ever had that honor. This lefthander has been one of Minnesota's most consistent pitchers the past two seasons.

PLACE CORRECT STICKER HERE

Answer:_____

2 An established relief pitcher with the Mets and Expos for eight seasons, this righthander was dealt to Minnesota in 1987. He has solidified the Twins' bullpen ever since.

PLACE CORRECT STICKER HERE

Answer:_____

3 A hometown boy, this lefthanded-hitting slugger is annually among the club leaders in homers and RBIs. A shoulder injury hampered him in 1989.

PLACE
CORRECT
STICKER
HERE

Answer:_____

4 Easily one of the major leagues' most exciting performers, this hustling outfielder hits for both average and power. He has gained All Star team status in each of the past four years.

PLACE
CORRECT
STICKER
HERE

Answer:_____

Did You Know...

Hall of Famer Harmon Killebrew hit 475 of his 573 career home runs, including eight grand-slammers, for the Minnesota Twins from 1961 through 1974.

TRIVIA QUIZ

OAKLAND
A'S

Answers on page 94

1 An American League batting champion with Boston in 1981, this righthand-hitting infielder has been one of the Athletics' most consistent performers for the past seven years.

PLACE
CORRECT
STICKER
HERE

Answer: _____

2 A wrist injury limited him for the first part of last year. His home run and basestealing talents made him the Most Valuable Player in the American League in 1988.

PLACE
CORRECT
STICKER
HERE

Answer: _____

3 The American League's top rookie in 1987 set a home run record for freshmen. This tall, righthanded slugger hit over 100 fourbaggers in just two and a half seasons.

PLACE
CORRECT
STICKER
HERE

Answer: _____

4 A veteran with previous success in Cleveland and Boston, this side-arming righthander became a relief specialist for the A's in 1987. He has become one of the game's premier firemen.

PLACE
CORRECT
STICKER
HERE

Answer: _____

Did You Know...

Oakland A's manager Tony LaRussa holds a law degree. He is only the fifth skipper in major league history to hold that distinction.

TRIVIA QUIZ

SEATTLE
MARINERS

Answers on page 94

1 His plate production as a rookie last year indicated this kid is the successful son of a famous father. His dad, incidentally, was an active performer in the National League last year.

PLACE
CORRECT
STICKER
HERE

Answer: _____

2 Despite missing June with injured knee ligaments, this rapidly improving catcher displayed offensive punch and demonstrated defense and a fine throwing arm.

PLACE
CORRECT
STICKER
HERE

Answer: _____

3 He became one of the American League's premier relief pitchers in only his second full season with the Mariners. The club drafted him in the second round of the June 1985 draft.

PLACE
CORRECT
STICKER
HERE

Answer:_____

4 He was signed by the Mariners as a free agent in December 1988. This former National League outfielder-turned-designated-hitter produced home run and RBI numbers that won him a spot on the All Star team.

PLACE
CORRECT
STICKER
HERE

Answer:_____

Did You Know...

In their 14 seasons in the American League, the Seattle Mariners have never won a divisional title nor celebrated an MVP award performer or a Cy Young Award winner.

TRIVIA QUIZ

TEXAS RANGERS

Answers on page 94

1 Baseball's all-time strike-out king, this 43-year-old speedball pitcher defies all baseball laws by continuing to perform at an amazing pace.

PLACE
CORRECT
STICKER
HERE

Answer: _____

2 This Dominican-born infielder was acquired from Cleveland in December 1988. He hit over .300 for the fourth straight year and in 1989 reached the American League All Star team.

PLACE
CORRECT
STICKER
HERE

Answer: _____

3 Part of a nine-player swap with the Cubs in December 1988, this lefthanded-hitting outfielder-first baseman made himself right at home in his first year with the Rangers.

PLACE CORRECT STICKER HERE

Answer: _____

4 Originally the property of Cincinnati, this right-hander made the All Star team in 1988 and 1989. He blossomed into a super relief ace with the Rangers and has been piling up saves.

PLACE CORRECT STICKER HERE

Answer: _____

Did You Know...

Jeff Burroughs, who played for the Texas Rangers from 1972 to 1976, was the American League's MVP in 1974. He is the only Ranger ever to win that award.

Red with Phil Rizzuto, New York Yankees announcer.

YOU MAKE THE CALL

Is the batter out when he bunts a pitch, drops his bat in fair ground, and the ball rebounds and bounces against the bat?

Not necessarily. It's an umpire's judgment. If he rules there was no intentional interference, the ball is in play. However, if the umpire decides it was intentional, the batter is out and no other runners may advance.

Is a batter out if he slides safely into first base and his momentum carries him past the bag?

No, a batter can't be tagged out when he overslides first base, providing he returns immediately to that base.

What constitutes running out of the baseline?

A runner is out when he goes more than three feet from a direct line between bases to avoid a tag, unless he does so to avoid interfering with a defensive player trying to field a batted ball.

What happens when a batter, not trying to swing at a pitch, is struck by a pitched ball?

He's entitled to first base unless the pitch was in the strike zone when it contacted him. Then it's a strike. If it wasn't in the strike zone but the batter made no effort to avoid being hit, the umpire will call the pitch a ball.

What happens when a fielder, chasing a fly ball, reaches over a fence or railing and a spectator pulls the glove off his hand, preventing him from making a catch?

No fan interference is called when a player does this. However, the batter can be called out for fan interference if a spectator reaches across a fence or railing to hinder a fielder trying to make a catch.

What happens when a batter disputes a called strike and then refuses to return to the batter's box at the umpire's order?

The umpire can direct the pitcher to throw the ball, and until the hitter reenters the box, he may call every pitch a strike. The batter may return to the box, but if he doesn't do so before three strikes are called, he's out.

BASEBALL SCRAMBLERS

Unscramble the letters below to find the names of things you might *see, hear,* or *need* when you spend a day at the ballpark. Write the words you find in the boxes beside the scrambled letters. Copy the circled letter in the numbered blue box beside the word. (To start you off, we've done the first scramble.) When you've solved all 22 scrambles, use the numbered letters to reveal a SECRET MESSAGE.

TAMSUID — S T A D I U (M)   1 M

TICSEKT — □□□○□□□   2

PPO LYF — □○□ □□□   3

NUBT — ○□□□   4

RESCO — □□○□□   5

RETCHIP — □□□□□○□   6

NILE VIRED — ○□□□ □□□□□   7

TUGDOU — □□□□□○   8

HOCCA — □□○□□   9

KITERS — □□□□□○   10

BRETTA — □□□○□□   11

92

LOFU LABL

MIREUP

EBAS THI

REROR

EBASBALL

DIELS

OTH ODG

FOULTIED

EMOH URN

RETHACC

GRAMNEA

12 ___
13 ___
14 ___
15 ___
16 ___
17 ___
18 ___
19 ___
20 ___
21 ___
22 ___

Fill in the letters from the numbered boxes above, in the matching numbered boxes below, to reveal the SECRET MESSAGE.

Answers on page 95

| 11 | 21 | 2 | 16 | | 20 | 15 | | 5 | 13 | 8 | | 19 | 3 |

| 14 | 18 | 10 | | 4 | 12 | 17 | 7 | 22 | 9 | 1 | 6 |

93

ANSWERS TO TRIVIA QUIZ

Chicago Cubs
Mark Grace
Andre Dawson
Mitch Williams
Jerome Walton
Montreal Expos
Tim Wallach
Andres Galarraga
Tim Burke
Mark Langston
New York Mets
Darryl Strawberry
Randy Myers
Kevin McReynolds
Dwight Gooden
Philadelphia Phillies
Von Hayes
Len Dykstra
Steve Jeltz
Tom Herr
Pittsburgh Pirates
Andy Van Slyke
Barry Bonds
Glenn Wilson
Doug Drabek
St. Louis Cardinals
Vince Coleman
Jose DeLeon
Pedro Guerrero
Ozzie Smith
Atlanta Braves
Dale Murphy
Lonnie Smith
John Smoltz
Tom Glavine
Cincinnati Reds
John Franco
Eric Davis
Barry Larkin
Paul O'Neill
Houston Astros
Glenn Davis
Jim Deshaies
Mike Scott
Dave Smith

Los Angeles Dodgers
Eddie Murray
Orel Hershiser
Jay Howell
Mike Morgan
San Diego Padres
Tony Gwynn
Benito Santiago
Jack Clark
Mark Davis
San Francisco Giants
Will Clark
Kevin Mitchell
Brett Butler
Rick Reuschel
Baltimore Orioles
Cal Ripken, Jr.
Mickey Tettleton
Jeff Ballard
Gregg Olson
Boston Red Sox
Wade Boggs
Mike Greenwell
Ellis Burks
Roger Clemens
Cleveland Indians
Joe Carter
Cory Snyder
Greg Swindell
Scott Bailes
Detroit Tigers
Lou Whitaker
Guillermo Hernandez
Matt Nokes
Alan Trammell
Milwaukee Brewers
Paul Molitor
Rob Deer
Dan Plesac
Chris Bosio
New York Yankees
Don Mattingly
Steve Sax
Dave Righetti
Jesse Barfield

Toronto Blue Jays
Jimmy Key
Kelly Gruber
Tony Fernandez
Fred McGriff
California Angels
Lance Parrish
Bryan Harvey
Devon White
Bert Blyleven
Chicago White Sox
Carlton Fisk
Ron Kittle
Ivan Calderon
Bobby Thigpen
Kansas City Royals
George Brett
Kevin Seitzer
Bo Jackson
Steve Farr
Minnesota Twins
Alan Anderson
Jeff Reardon
Kent Hrbek
Kirby Puckett
Oakland A's
Carney Lansford
Jose Canseco
Mark McGwire
Dennis Eckersley
Seattle Mariners
Ken Griffey, Jr.
Dave Valle
Mike Schooler
Jeffrey Leonard
Texas Rangers
Nolan Ryan
Julio Franco
Rafael Palmeiro
Jeff Russell

BASEBALL SCRAMBLERS

1 M	2 K	3 O	4 B	5 O	6 E	7 L	8 T	9 A	10 E	11 T

TAMSUID S T A D I (U) M

TICSEKT T I (C) K E T S

PPO LYF P O P F L Y

NUBT (B) U N T

RESCO S C (O) R E

RETCHIP P I T C H E R

NILE VIRED (L) I N E D R I V E

TUGDOU D U G O U (T)

HOCCA C O A C H

KITERS S T R I K (E)

BRETTA B A T (T) E R

12 A	13 U	14 T	15 E	16 E	17 L	18 H	19 T	20 I	21 A	22 G

LOFU LABL F O U L B A L L

MIREUP (U) M P I R E

EBAS THI B A S E H I (T)

REROR (E) R R O R

EBASBALL B A S (E) B A L L

DIELS S L I D (E)

OTH ODG (H) O T D O G

FOULTIED O U T F I E L D

EMOH URN H O M (E) R U N

RETHACC (C) A T C H E R

GRAMNEA M A N A G E R

T A K E M E O U T T O
11 21 2 16 20 15 5 13 8 19 3

T H E B A L L G A M E
14 18 10 4 12 17 7 22 9 1 6

MAJOR LEAGUE TEAM CITIES — ANSWERS

NATIONAL LEAGUE TEAMS
1. New York Mets
2. Philadelphia Phillies
3. Pittsburgh Pirates
4. Montreal Expos
5. Chicago Cubs
6. St. Louis Cardinals
7. Houston Astros
8. Los Angeles Dodgers
9. Atlanta Braves
10. San Francisco Giants
11. Cincinnati Reds
12. San Diego Padres

AMERICAN LEAGUE TEAMS
1. New York Yankees
2. Boston Red Sox
3. Chicago White Sox
4. Cleveland Indians
5. Detroit Tigers
6. Milwaukee Brewers
7. Minnesota Twins — city Minneapolis
8. Kansas City Royals
9. Baltimore Orioles
10. Texas Rangers — city Arlington
11. Oakland A's
12. Seattle Mariners
13. California Angels — city Anaheim
14. Toronto Blue Jays

ANSWERS TO BASEBALL TERMINOLOGY

Hot corner — Third base
High heat — Rising fastball
Uncle Charlie — A good curveball. Dwight Gooden's is called Lord Charles
Chin music — High inside pitch thrown to intimidate a batter
Hot dog — Player who tends to show off a bit while making a play
A laugher — Winning an easy game by piling up an early lead
Good wheels — Player who can run
Good hose — Player or pitcher with a good arm
Scroogie — Also called a screwball pitch
Play by the book — When a manager plays the game conservatively
Gopher ball — A home run that will "go for" distance
Grapefruit League — Spring exhibition games in Florida
Cactus League — Spring exhibition games in Arizona
Can of corn — High, lazy flyball to outfield
Band box — Small ballpark in which a lot of home runs are hit
Take him Downtown — What a hitter does to a pitcher when he hits a homer
Couldn't find the handle — When a fielder bobbles a ball
Pulled the string — When a pitcher fools a hitter with a slow pitch
Turn the ball over — When a pitcher, generally a lefty, turns wrist inward
Splitter — The split-finger pitch currently so popular
Wet one up — When a pitcher throws a spitball
Texas Leaguer — Soft fly that falls between infield and outfield
A flare — A base hit similar to a Texas Leaguer
A leg hit — When a batter beats out a groundball to the infield
He roped one — When a batter gets a hard, linedrive base hit
Having a good eye — A hitter who takes close pitches that are called balls